Secrets to Living in the Secret Place

LEARNING TO WALK IN THE ABIDING PRESENCE OF GOD

Barbara A. Michael

Secrets to Living in the Secret Place
Learning to Walk in the Abiding Presence of God
Copyright © 2020 by Barbara A. Michael

All rights reserved. No part of this book may be reproduced or transmitted in any form or by any means without written permission from the author.

"Scripture taken from the New King James Version. Copyright © 1982 by Thomas Nelson, Inc. Used by permission. All rights reserved."

Published by

www.speaktruthmedia.com

Cover Photo by: Dave Hoefler on Unsplash
Cover design by: SpeakTruth Media Group LLC
Author photo by: Leslie Kinney

ISBN 978-1-7342646-4-7 *(pb)*
Printed in USA

Dedication

To my Mom and Dad who taught me that, what is important in life, is not the things we can buy, but the relationships God blesses us with.

As our family grew and began to spread out miles apart, Mom, with a passion to write and a fervency for the family unit, published monthly newsletters to help us all stay in touch. Later, her and Dad together began creating greeting cards for the family.

I remember as a child watching Mom and believe the strength I now have to write was nurtured by seeing her determination as she sat at her typewriter creating articles and short stories. Then later having these monthly newsletters and specially made greeting cards show up in my mail box.

Thank you, Mom and Dad, for the best upbringing.

I love you forever!

CONTENTS

Introduction 7
What is the Secret Place? 11
Making Time Alone with God a Priority 14
The Secret Place of our Prayer Closet 18
Dwelling & Abiding 24
Location Changes 26
The Presence of God 29
His Presence is Our Source 36
The Communion of the Holy Spirit 41
From a Prayer Life to a Life of Prayer 46
His Word, Our Guide 50
Responding to God 55
The Joyful Process 62
Closing 65
About the Author 68

Introduction

One thing I have desired of the Lord, that will I seek:
That I may dwell in the house of the Lord
all the days of my life, to behold
the beauty of the Lord and to inquire in His temple.
For in the time of trouble He shall hide me in His pavilion;
In the secret place of His tabernacle He shall hide me;
He shall set me high upon a rock. (Ps 27:4 & 5)

Though chaos may surround us, the peace of God never leaves us! Can you imagine living that way with the everlasting peace of God?

It is probably safe to say that we all desire to have a sense of inner peace and strength that keeps us steady even in times of uncertainty. It is possible! Not only is it possible, but it is also the way we were created to live. However, there is only one way to achieve this kind of life, and that's through a real relationship with God, our Father in heaven. We discover this blessed life once we make Jesus Christ our Lord and learn to spend time alone with God, in His presence where we find what's called in Scripture, "The Secret Place." In this place, a veil is removed, and God's existence is no longer an idea, an imagination, or a hopeful dream, but it becomes a reality.

In the Bible, there is a story of a man named Moses and how he had encounters with God that caused him to want to never be without the presence of God. For anyone who has truly experienced the presence of God, the impact can leave us with the same desire. We find God is not someone to be afraid of but rather One to embrace and cling to every day.

The peace that comes from a close relationship with God is a peace that is unshakeable. It's relentless against the pressing fears of the world around us. No matter what is going on, what noise you hear, what trouble you face, what calamity the world around you is in an uproar about, this peace that flows from a close relationship with God is a deep well within, formed through our encounters with God in the secret place. This peace takes dominion in adversity to not only keep us but also to demonstrate the love of God to others with the intent to draw them to Christ, so they too can experience the life God intends for them.

Any experience we have in life is eternal. It never goes away. You can't undo something that is done. But how you allow it to impact you is up to you. Experiencing the presence of God can awaken in us a desire to never be without Him actively involved in our life. In His presence, we can discover the peace and rest that is sought after by every human being but found only by those who embrace the opportunity God gives them to get to know Him. If we embrace this opportunity by opening our lives to God, we will find He is real, He is good, and He will keep us in His care if we let Him.

Through our encounters with God in our times spent alone with Him, we can learn to live in this secret place of His presence. What goes on in that time alone with God is between you and God. There, we can remove our masks and pretenses and be heart to heart real with Him. He knows everything about us, understands it all, and yearns to spend time with us. He wants to pour His love for us over all that we are.

As long as we keep wearing masks, thinking we are hiding who we really are, we are holding ourselves back from God and from the peace found in His presence. Once we've received Jesus Christ as Lord, His fullness is available to us, but we must draw near to God and allow ourselves to get to know Him. When we unveil ourselves before God with honesty, surrendering to Him, He welcomes us with open arms, inviting us to come closer and closer to Him. He wants us to experience the depth of Who He is. He wants us to be deeply acquainted with Him. As we continue to respond to Him with a, "Yes Lord," we find we have entered a relationship that will ultimately become the most powerful force in our lives.

He is the Source of everything we will ever need and can take all that we have become, through the ups and downs, and transform our lives into the most fulfilling life we could ever imagine. As we continue cultivating our relationship with God, we become so immersed in Who He is that we become hidden in Him. As we remain in Him, His goodness and grace overflow into every area of our life. But, it begins in the secret place of His presence.

It is in humble service to God that I have written this book. As I waited on God to hear what He would say, I experienced a degree of His love for you that compelled me to do my best to serve Him in His purpose. As He led me to share, even from some of my personal experiences with Him, it was with fear and trembling I penned the words. Though I may not know who you are, God's intentions for you as you read this book were strong upon my heart. If you hunger to know God and live in close communion with Him, I hope this book will help ignite a fire in you to run into the secret place of His presence and find Him. And that in that place, you allow Him to transform and guide you in a never-ending walk with Him, that establishes the inner peace and strength that nothing will ever be able to take from you.

Let's begin!

CHAPTER ONE

What is the Secret Place?

He who dwells in the secret place of the Most High shall abide under the shadow of the Almighty. (Psalm 91:1)

The secret place is a place of communion with God, where we are more aware of Him and His greatness than the challenges we face daily. It's a place established by our times of solitude with God. There, in His presence, a powerful union is formed that compels us to find a way to abide in Him. Living in this place of communion with God keeps us near Him no matter where we are or what is going on. One of my favorite Scripture verses in the Bible comes from Psalm 91, verse one above.

The *"Almighty"* is God, the Supreme One. There is no one higher or greater than God. The *"secret place"* is like a hiding place in His presence where He covers us with His "shadow." Here He keeps us through every sort of situation or circumstance life could throw our way. To *abide under the shadow of the Almighty* means we stay in that place where God keeps us covered.

This ability to abide in Him starts in the secret place of what the Bible calls a closet or room (Matthew 6:6). It's the place where you and God meet for private prayer. You may have a favorite quiet spot in your home or a unique chair where you spend time in devotion. Perhaps your car is a place where you pray. The key is that you are alone and focused on a conversation with the Lord your God. Here we can get to know God in a real personal way, and that's where the abiding in Him begins.

Have you ever had days when you consecutively spent quiet time with the Lord and became consumed with thoughts of Him and aware of His involvement in every aspect of your life? There are times when we feel so close to God that we don't want anything else to get our attention. We have determined that we do not want to live one moment without an awareness that His presence is with us. So, what do you do when you recognize this desire in you to stay close to Him?

Have you ever made a sincere decision to spend regular quality time with God but are faithful for only a few days before everything else fills your time? As a result, you feel empty and wonder how that happened. You see, as we cultivate our relationship with God, we find we have great intentions but are not always faithful to follow through to accomplish our goals. The key is don't quit when you fall short of your plans or when things don't go as you expected. Good relationships take time, and this powerful union with

God is worth the time. Invest your time into the secret place. Let the richness of your experiences in His presence spur you on to the more He has for you. Keep putting effort toward Him, again and again, until you become so attached to God that you cannot live without Him. It will be worth it!

    Now I'd like to share some secrets with you that help me learn to live in the secret place of God's abiding presence.

CHAPTER TWO

Making Time Alone with God a Priority

*Now in the morning, having risen
a long while before daylight, He went out and departed
to a solitary place; and there He prayed.* (Mark 1:35 & 36)

One of the secrets to living in the secret place is making time alone with God a priority.

I do not mean just putting it at the top of our want-to-do list, but seriously making it a must-do necessity in our daily life. If we settle it in our mind that time alone with God is as essential as the air we breathe, then we will decide we must do it. Once we make our decision, it will take effort on our part to follow through. But, there is absolutely nothing in life more important than spending time with the One who created you, knows your future, and Who has plans for your life that are beyond what you could even dream of today.

If we have a habit of meeting with God, our time together will affect every area of our life. And, we will notice that our experience during those times become alive in us throughout our day. The same heart we have in our time alone with God is preserved in us as we give attention to the outward things of our life. We are not one way when alone with God, and different when our time is given to other things.

Even though we are not sitting somewhere in a time of private prayer with God, we are thinking of Him and the relationship we have with Him. The more we get to know God, the more our thoughts are toward Him. Somehow along the way, we find that no matter where we are or who we are with, our contemplations are on God. We begin filtering everything through our relationship with Him, as we think of His perspective before responding to anything.

Spending time alone with God changes our focus and helps us learn to keep our attention on Him. We are creating and establishing a habit that will ultimately become our lifestyle. Then we find that in every situation, our heart is toward God, and we are looking and listening for Him as we do the things we do.

As we interact with others, we consider what God thinks about what we hear and see. We want to listen to what He has to say about everything. We want to please Him. So, we go to Him for everything: every decision, word, and action. Asking, should we speak or be quiet and certainly how do we pray.

No matter what we are exposed to, there is this inner communion with God going on that guides and directs us and prompts us into action, whether quietly in prayer or outwardly in some form of service to others. As we begin to operate this way, we are living in the secret place of His presence. Our outward actions are influenced by our inward communion with God. This communion is ignited in our times alone with Him.

We have great examples recorded in the Bible that demonstrate the importance of making time alone with God a priority.

Jesus started His days in prayer alone with the Father. Not only did He begin the day that way, but He often withdrew from the crowds of people He was ministering to, in order to spend time alone with the Father. You see, people continually needed and sought the power of God that flowed from Jesus. His union with the Father was the Source of that power. Time alone with Him was a must. Do you know people who need God's involvement in their life? Like Jesus, if we spend time with the Father, His power will flow from our union with Him and make a difference in the lives of others. Here are just a few references to Jesus' daily need for time alone with the Father.

> Jesus went up the mountain by Himself
> to pray. (Matthew 14:23)

> Early in the morning, Jesus departed
> to a solitary place and prayed. (Mark 1:35)

> Jesus Himself often withdrew into the wilderness
> and prayed. (Luke 5:16)

Another example of making time alone with God a priority is seen in the life of Moses. After leading God's people out of Egypt, crossing the Red Sea, and arriving at Mount Sanai, the first thing he did was go up the mountain to meet with God

(Exodus Chapters 12 thru 19). Moses was to lead a whole nation of people through the wilderness as God directed him. His time alone with God was essential. It was his first priority!

Making time alone with God a priority will change our lives completely. Here we begin to live in the secret place with Him.

CHAPTER THREE

The Secret Place of our Prayer Closet

*But you, when you pray, go into your room,
and when you have shut your door, pray to your Father
who is in the secret place; and your Father who sees in secret will reward
you openly.* (Matt. 6:6)

If you asked me, "What is Prayer?" I would have answered, "There is no way to give a full description of what prayer is." In part, prayer is something that acknowledges a need and turns to God for its fulfillment. A need can be anything from a specific physical need to the need for wisdom, understanding, or spiritual insight in a situation. The greatest need, of course, is our need for a close relationship with God.

In simplicity, prayer is communication with the Lord our God that takes on many forms like prayers of salvation, consecration, dedication, request, supplication, commitment, forgiveness, declaration, and many more. Prayer is sometimes the silent attention of the heart to God while waiting for His instruction. There is no limit to what prayer can be, but it is communication with God who Himself is limitless.

There are times when praying with someone else, or a group of people is beneficial. We can pray with others in a small group of 2 or more people or with a whole company of people in large groups and assemblies. With technology these days, there are even ways of joining with others in prayer all around the world on our computers, cell phones, and other devices. It's amazing!

There are times, however, when our prayers need to be done privately with the Lord, which is what I call the secret place of our prayer closet. Here, we meet alone with God for private prayer.

In private prayer with God, it is only you and Him. In this place of privacy, through conversation, worship, reading, and studying of the Bible, etc., we develop our relationship with God, our Father. Here we learn about Him and become acquainted with His presence, sometimes just sitting quietly in this place with Him. During these times, we find we can trust Him and unveil our soul to Him with complete transparency. In 2 Corinthians 3:18, we learn that when we spend time in this place with God, He can heal, nurture, and transform our life into a beautiful and enjoyable relationship with Him.

This place of solitude is like a quarry or a place of transformation mentioned in 1 Kings 6:7. Stones used to build the Temple in Solomon's day were finished in the quarry so that no hammer or chisel or any iron tool was heard at the Temple while it was being built.

There was a finishing work to be done with the quarry stones before they could be of use to build the Temple. The quarry provided the necessary room and the proper equipment to bring out the beauty of the stone. We are like the stones found in the quarry. When we begin to pursue a deep relationship with God, we are just as life has made us and in great need of the working of God's love and care.

Have you ever heard the term "a diamond in the rough?" It simply means that the diamond is not yet refined, just like the quarry stone. In the stone's unrefined state, they were unfit for use to build the Temple. Each had to be cut and shaped to make it ready for construction.

Like the stones, there is an intricate work to be done in our lives that can only happen in the secret place of our prayer closet. Like in the quarry, the deep, intricate, and sometimes painful yet liberating work that God does in our soul and character must be done. Our private prayer closet gives us a place to be transparent. There we can be free and honest as we share with our Father, God, about everything. Yes, everything, even every ugly, painful, heart-wrenching thing we have experienced.

God can do in us and for us what no one else can. He will help us let go of past disappointments, mistreatments, sorrows, and any other thing that tries to hold us in a place of captivity. If we carry all our pain and sorrow with us wherever we go, it will keep us from enjoying fulfilling relationships. We live life like a rollercoaster, one day almost happy and the next sad and disappointed. Ultimately, we can become miserable.

I've heard it said: "Misery loves company." Sometimes people who are miserable don't want to, or don't know how to, deal with troubling things by taking them to the Father in prayer. As a result, they have a tendency to want the people around them to be miserable too. When others don't join in the misery, they are considered enemies and relationships are broken or hindered because of it.

You see, without God, we live in the limits of our human nature, which can be destructive. If we do not allow the love of God to work in us, when someone hurts us, disappoints us, mistreats us, or just doesn't live up to our expectations, we tend to hold a grudge against them. Then to protect ourselves, we vow never to let them or anyone mistreat us again, which is unrealistic.

It is so easy to misunderstand someone and build a big case against them based on what we think happened or we think they did or meant by whatever they did. And there are times when people are badly mistreated. These kinds of experiences can cause us to build walls of resistance in our life and let the pain of mistreatment fester in us to the point that what comes out of us is anger, fear, and abuse towards others. If these things continue in our life, it can lead to not only destruction in our life but also those around us.

However, in the secret place of God's presence, like in the quarry, through conversation and communion with God, He can chip away all our hardness and heal all our sorrows and make us free to love ourselves and others. As God heals all of our pain, peace, joy, and strength will come bursting forth with a newfound ability to love ourselves, love others, and enable us to have enjoyable quality relationships.

If you are in a place of misery, please seek God. Tell Him how you are hurting. Tell Him you don't want to hurt anymore and ask Him for His help. He will not refuse you! You may even want to ask Him to direct you to a friend, a minister or Christian counselor who can help you work through things and help you press into God and learn of His healing love.

If you will keep coming to God in prayer and make the most of the opportunities He places before you to learn about His way of doing things, you will, step by step, become freer and freer of all the stuff that has tried to crush you and snuff you out.

The chisel, hammer, and iron tools God uses in the secret place of private prayer are comforting, cleansing, caring, creative, healing, and restorative. He shows you how to confront your sorrows with the Word of God in a way that will gently hammer down your walls, chip away the hard spots, and produce the beauty of who you are – a lovely display of God's creative power and love.

I've heard of a great artist, Leonardo da Vinci, who never saw a piece of stone like it was but like it could be with an artisan's touch. As he took his hammer and chisel to a piece of rock, he gently and precisely chipped away at the stone with such love, vision, and care to produce beautiful works of art.

Remember, private prayer is time alone with God, where it's only you and Him. There you are safe, and what goes on in that time is between you and God. He is pouring His love over you, and it is a transforming power that can heal all your brokenness, wash away your impurities, and make you brand new, ready for His purpose.

Our prayer closet is like a quarry with God, where He forms us into valuable vessels useful for His building of the church. As we cultivate our relationship with Him in these times, He also transforms the way we relate to others. What He does in our soul will give us the ability to love others past any flaws they may demonstrate. Because we have personally experienced God's mercy and patience, we can extend the same to others. We understand the need for love and the power of it. As we walk in His love towards others, we will not only experience a significant level of peace and strength but will see God use our peace and strength to draw others to Christ.

Oh, what joy it is to live in the secret place!

CHAPTER FOUR

Dwelling & Abiding

Blessed are those who dwell in Your house;
They will still be praising You. (Ps. 84:4)

Since living in the secret place begins by establishing a meeting place for private prayer with God, then let's consider how we create our place of meeting.

Our key Scripture Psalm 91:1 can help us gain understanding. The psalmist wrote, "He who dwells in the secret place of the Most High, shall abide under the shadow of the Almighty." In the original Hebrew language, to "dwell" meant to sit down in quiet, to remain, to settle, to marry, make to abide, continue, establish, habitation, make to inhabit, and make to keep. And, to "abide" means to stop and stay permanently.

Keep these definitions in mind while establishing your personal secret place where you meet with God and use them to understand the communion you carry with you from your private prayer closet.

Start by finding a specific location where you can meet with God. Remember, though, establishing a set area doesn't mean we can't talk with God unless we are in that real place. It is just a specific meeting place designated to help us develop our communion with Him. In that location, you can sit down in quiet, settle in, and begin your time with the Lord.

At first, you may wonder what to do, or you might begin to speak with God right away, then find your time of prayer complete in a matter of minutes. Don't be overly concerned with what you do or how long you spend there. As you continue to meet with Him every day, you will find it easier to commune with Him. Your times of private prayer will become the most enriching part of your life.

I love the two phrases that define "dwell," make to inhabit and to keep. Inhabit simply means to occupy and keep means to retain possession. As you build your place of prayer, make it with an intent to take up occupancy of that place and keep it as an exclusive possession for you to meet with God.

In this physical place of prayer, we are forming a spiritual union with the Father, done to learn to dwell and abide in Him. The things that unfold as you are establishing your meeting place with God happen to bring a permanent change in how you live your life. We learn to make our heart a dwelling place for God, and we find we want to abide in an ongoing relationship with Him.

CHAPTER FIVE

Location Changes

How lovely is Your tabernacle, O Lord of hosts!
My soul longs, yes, even faints for the courts of the Lord;
My heart and my flesh cry out for the living God. (Ps. 84:1 & 2)

Our meeting place can change from time to time based on our life seasons. For example, when my husband and I were raising our children, the house was busy with homeschooling, their activities, and our business. And with all that, my husband was in and out of the home at different times during the day. It was quite a challenge to find a quiet place to have time alone with God.

We were remodeling our home to add space that would meet the needs of our family. The unfinished area was full of required construction materials for the completion of the room. At times throughout the day, I would slip into that room, away from all the household busyness, hoping no one would think to look for me there as I spent time with God.

Sometimes it was only a few minutes, but it was my established meeting place with God in that season of my life.

I think it is interesting now that when we finished the room addition, later, it became our master bedroom, and my specific meeting place turned out to be our walk-in closet. For many years I kept the closet as my secret place with God. When I couldn't find a quiet place or the prayers that were on my heart to pray required a hidden place, I would go into the closet. Yes, it was full of clothes, but it was also my prayer closet, and any time I went there to meet God, He was waiting and ready to hear from me. Oh, the things that were accomplished over the years in that place of prayer.

If we have an established place to meet with God whenever we go there, it is easier to settle our hearts. We know this is where we meet with God, and we are ready to be quiet with Him, to pray, to talk, to read the Word, and to let Him speak. All the things that go on in that secret place with Him are so special.

As life seasons change, we can start feeling the shift long before anything happens. I remember a time when I experienced an unsettledness in my heart. I felt agitated and didn't understand why. I was talking with a friend, and as we inquired of God together, she helped me see what was going on.

We were preparing to move out of our home of almost 30 years, a place where much had been accomplished. My heart for ministry was changing too, and I was feeling an expansion. A work of God was taking place as He prepared me for the next phase of His purpose for my life. I was serving full-time as an associate pastor at a church, but what God was asking me to do would require me to resign from that office of the ministry to move into the next season.

I had a private office at the church, and it had become a secret place of prayer for me where I met with God before meeting with anyone else or participating in any form of ministry. Much of my responsibility there was to oversee the church's prayer ministry. My office was also attached to the prayer room, where I led prayer several times every week. Resigning meant I would have to give up this cherished place of prayer, which was heart-wrenching for me. My friend helped me realize that I felt unsettled because I was being uprooted from two important places in my life. There is tremendous significance in having a place to meet in private with God.

On top of those two life-changes, I didn't have a home yet to move into where I could create my new place of prayer. I was unsettled because I felt like I had no place to meet with God. It was like not having a place to live and breathe, so I sought the Lord about it and found out what to do.

It was time to establish a new meeting place, but we were in transition. We were remodeling our new home, and it would take several months for completion. So, I began making trips to the house when no one was there to sit in the quietness of that place as I met with God. Months later, when we moved in, my meeting place with God was already established, and His presence was there.

Through that experience, I learned it is vital for me to have a place where I can meet with God. Even when I'm traveling, when I arrive, the first thing I do is search for a place where I can be alone with God. Without it, I am so unsettled. But once I find the place, I am good to go.

CHAPTER SIX

The Presence of God

And He said, "My Presence will go with you, and I will give you rest." (Ex. 33:14)

We become acquainted with God's presence when we spend time alone with Him. As we encounter Him, we begin to know Him in a real tangible way. I am talking about having an awareness of the pure majesty of who God is. He is Holy. He is pure, right, just, majestic, almighty, and so much more. He is everything good, right, and perfect. He loves us without measure or restraint, and He wants us to know He is with us.

When God's presence is with us, we are encompassed about by His almightiness, which is a safe and secure place. We can see all through the Scripture where the presence of God is with His people. We are His people, and He wants us to live in the secret place of His presence as we live out our days here on earth.

Look at these examples in the Scripture of God's presence with those who are His. In the Book of Exodus, you can follow

Moses' life and see how God's presence was with him. In Exodus 33:7-14, we see God came near to Moses and spoke with him and promised His presence would go with him. Psalm 46 tells us that God is with us and is a very present help. In Matthew 28:18–20, Jesus speaks to His disciples, instructing them to go and teach everyone everywhere about the things of God and tells them He will be with them always. Jesus' words are for everyone who has chosen to give their lives to Him and follow Him.

As we spend time with God in private prayer, reading His Word, and communing with Him, we become more acquainted with Him. We get to know Him. Who He is, how He is, His character, and what pleases Him. We find He is more enjoyable than we ever imagined. We become consumed with thoughts of Him and begin to consider Him more and more in our daily activities. His involvement in our life increases, and we notice we have a heightened awareness of His presence with us.

In the privacy of our prayer closet, we can experience a degree of God's presence that makes us want to be aware of His presence with us everywhere we go. As we move from that private place of prayer into daily activities, we have to learn to stay mindful of Him. That takes practice, but God will help us if we sincerely want to keep our minds stayed on Him. I have noticed God doing things to get my attention so that I will remember He is with me. It's like His presence shows up reminding me that we have a relationship that matters to Him.

When someone you've spent a lot of time with and know very well walks into a room, you become aware of their presence, and you automatically have thoughts of them as to who they are and how they are with you in a relationship. You know them. You may even adjust your actions or focus as they enter the room. You have honor and respect for them based on what you know them to be. When it is someone you have a good relationship with, there is comfort, peace, and joy that comes over you because they are there.

In those times, when God's presence shows up, I am reminded of His desire to be involved in every area of my life, and my heart opens more to Him. I acknowledge His presence and welcome His communion. As I do, His presence becomes more tangible, and I have great peace because I know He is with me and will guide and keep me.

Think about how you respond to someone you enjoy being around. As you spend time with the person, you get to know them more. When you leave, you continue to think of them.

I recently spent a few days on a little getaway with two of my friends. We spent much time together in conversation and fellowship; we ate our meals together, prayed together, studied the Bible together, went on little outings, laughed, and had a good time. In all these activities, we learned more about each other, and our relationship was enriched as a result. When our time together ended and we parted ways, I couldn't help but continue to think of them, and for days, my thoughts were so much on them. As I thought about the conversations we had and the things we enjoyed together, I loved them even more! A higher degree of appreciation and care for them developed in my heart. I can't wait to spend time with them again. Real relationships feel and look like that, and we have that same opportunity with God.

Now, with God, He is always with us. We never have to part from Him. We do have to go out of our private prayer closet, but we can continue to fellowship with Him as we go and do the things we need to do. We learn to do something I refer to as courting His presence. We carry what takes place in our private time with Him with us wherever we go. There is a joy and a sense of peace because of our relationship with Him that affects how we handle other things in life. Like the time I spent with my friends, I carried joy from our time together into what I was doing next. I believe even the people I interacted with afterward felt that joy, and it was a pleasure being with me because of it. When we are pleasant, people like being around us.

You see, we should take the enjoyment of our relationship with God to others. What we receive from Him should spill into everything else we do. The key is to be aware of the attention of our hearts. When we notice we aren't so peaceful and positive, it's a signal that we need to put our focus on God again and get recharged by His presence.

I want to say a little more here about courting His presence. God wants us to be aware that His presence is always with us. We can live our life either with or without His help. If we live from the secret place of His presence, we can glean from His character and capabilities. As we acknowledge His presence, His attention is turned toward us even more. Sometimes just a whisper of thanksgiving and adoration for Him draws Him nearer to us. Like James wrote in Chapter four, verse eight, "Draw near to God, and He will draw near to you."

I remember a challenging situation I walked through one time. There was something specific I had to do that I wasn't looking forward to doing. I had put it off for quite some time because I couldn't bear to even think of it. The Lord would nudge me about it often. One day I realized it was time to take care of it. The Lord was again prompting me about it, and I wanted to obey. Suddenly I had the desire to take care of the matter and got it done that very day.

Afterward, I thought about how the experience unfolded and thanked God for how He was present every step of the way, speaking to my heart, instructing me, giving me understanding. And at times, it seemed He kept my soul from pain while healing the wounds that plagued me, even hindered me from moving forward.

When the task was completed, I noticed that He didn't just tell me to take care of it. He said, "Let's go take care of this." And we did! You see, I wasn't alone in it. My heart and soul were in His care the whole time, a beautiful example of the communion of God's presence, something we should never be without in our life. Oh, how God loves us!

Some things cannot be explained; you have to experience them for yourself. That is what spending time alone with God will do for you. You will experience Him, His presence, His love, His marvelous ways, personally for yourself.

What you need and what God has in store for you is for you alone, and no one else can lay hold of those things for you. As much as I can tell you about my relationship with God, I cannot make yours for you. I hope that what I share here will inspire you to find your place with God, as you court His presence. Please do not allow the unknown to stop you from approaching God and finding the extraordinary things He has for you.

For some reason, I grew up thinking I was not good enough. No matter what it pertained to, I always had this thought that I was not worthy to receive anything good. I believed a lie about myself that came straight from the devil, and I'm sure I'm not the only one who ever had a thought like that.

When I think about it now, I'm amazed I even went in search of a relationship with God. But that's how God loves us. He goes beyond what we can do or what we know, to reach us as He draws us to Christ.

Please know this truth, God keeps His promises and says in His Word that when we seek Him, we will find Him (Jeremiah 29:13). A sincere heart in search of God is irresistible to Him. When we set out to find God and know Him, He will make sure we find Him. He knows our hearts and allows us to see and experience who He is. So I say, "Seek Him all the more!" Even if you are afraid of what might happen, seek Him. You can trust Him. He will not harm you. He will pour out His love on you because He wants you to know His love and His presence.

God's Word also says, "We love Him because He first loved us" (1 John 4:19). He took the first step by giving His Son Jesus (John 3:16). Now He waits for our response. The thing is we cannot love Him until we discover that He loves us. So we shouldn't wait until we feel love for Him before we move towards Him. When we move towards Him, we find His love for us. He waits with great anticipation for us to respond. He waits with a longing in His heart that we will turn to Him in search of who He is. That longing in His heart is a powerful force that beckons our attention. He desires to bring us out of the death and destruction a life lived apart from Him will bring. As we grow in our comprehension of His great love, we can't help but love Him back.

God wants us to come closer and closer to Him so that He can show us more of His love. As we continue to spend time with Him, we will experience the depths of His love and learn more about the secret place of His presence. Oh, the presence of God, once experienced, awakens a longing within us to never be without Him. Those moments create a determination in us to live from the secret place of His presence.

Many of God's people settle for so much less than God intends for them. Some are satisfied by an occasional experience with Him, rather than putting effort into learning how to live in continual awareness of His holy presence. Please, my friends, do not reconcile yourself to live beneath what God intended for you. Seek to know Him, to know Him deeply like the Apostle Paul was determined to do (Philippians 3:8—10). Make time for personal experiences with God so that you recognize His presence and live encompassed by His love and care.

CHAPTER SEVEN

His Presence is Our Source

*I am the vine; you are the branches.
He who abides in Me, and I in him, bears much fruit;
for without Me you can do nothing.* (John 15:5)

Personally, when I began getting acquainted with God and developing a relationship with Him, it awakened something in me. As I continued to draw nearer to Him, I experienced His indescribable presence manifest in a way that set a course for my life. These moments caused me always to want to abide in Him and live from that secret place I found in Him—the place of His presence.

It became my regular practice to spend time drawing away from the things of my day-to-day life and drawing nearer to God. The attention of my heart and mind directed only to Him, expressing gratitude, devotion, and reverence to Him alone, sometimes for only moments other times for hours.

In these times of His manifest presence, a cultivation of my heart took place, transforming me from the inside out. I recognized I was self-centered. Through repentance and self-denial, I became less and less concerned about myself. The things I desired to do with my life changed. I handled things and related to others differently. Compassion for the well-being of others became more of my focus than the condition of my own life.

I soon recognized that these times in His presence became my Source of the peace God intended for me, well actually for all of us. I realized more and more the importance of spending time with God for no other reason than to express my heart in worship to Him. In these times, He draws so near that His presence engulfs us. As we recognize His majesty, our lives are forever changed.

The Word declares in Psalm 22:3 that God inhabits the praises of His people. And, we are to exalt the Lord our God and worship at His holy mountain, because "He is holy" (Psalm 99:9).

His presence in my life became something I couldn't live without anymore. I realized that apart from Him, I could do nothing. And frankly, I did not want even to try (John 15:5 & Exodus 33:12-15).

As my life's purpose unfolded and the outward ministry, He was calling me into manifested, it made demands of my time, which ultimately presented a challenge for me to hold onto my habit of spending regular time in this degree of His presence. Yet something in me, something God cultivated in me as we spent time together, would not allow me to go too far without recognizing I was missing something essential; time in His presence. Recently as I was adjusting to a new expansion in ministry, I experienced God's gentle yet stern warning not to forget Him.

My days are filled with family, ministry, and our business, so the responsibilities can be demanding. In seasons like this, if we are not careful, we can become consumed with the care of doing all these things and get overloaded. One day as I was wrestling to get a few minutes alone with God, something happened that turned my cares to victory. And, the experience reminded me of the essential need for time alone in God's presence.

It is my practice to start every day as Psalm 63:1 advises, "O God, You are my God, Early will I seek You." However, this particular day started unexpectedly and threw me out of my usual routine. Has that ever happened to you?

If we do not get to start our day in time alone with God, the day's events start demanding our attention. When this happens, we can find ourselves fighting against the increasing demands while we attempt to get quiet with the Lord. Remember, apart from God; we can do nothing.

I do not want to start my day without the awareness of God, for it is here that I yield my heart and mind to His supply of guidance and provision. The whole point of seeking God first in our day is to acknowledge our dependency on Him. As we acknowledge His Lordship and hear His heart, we are empowered by His Spirit to do what needs to be done that day.

Because of my cultivated union with God, I knew time alone with Him was vital. Even though on this day things started differently, I was determined to get to my place of prayer and give Him my undivided attention. Now, because the day's events were already making demands on me, I felt overburdened, and the longer it took to get to my place of prayer, the heavier my load of care seemed to be.

As I approached my place of prayer, I desired to give my full attention to God in a surrendered state of heart and mind, so I just fell on my face before Him in desperation. At this time, I was thinking I had to tell Him all about the load I was carrying and pray about all the issues people in my life were dealing with, instead, as soon as I bowed before Him, I heard Him say:

"All your time alone with Me does not have to be about everyone else. Remember to spend time with Me, for just you and Me."

When I heard this, I knew in my heart, He meant I was to do nothing at this moment with Him but worship Him. He alone is WORTHY!

He then led me in a three-minute exercise. He asked me to give Him three-minutes. I was to set a timer and worship Him as if I had no cares at all. It was to be just about Who He is.

Sounds easy, right?

Well, in those few minutes, my thoughts were challenged many times to go somewhere other than the worthiness of God. It hurts to admit that, because God is so worthy of our undivided attention, and my love for Him is so real, but cares were starting to take a place that belonged to Him. And He knew the danger of my variance from Him. He loves me so much that He led me through this exercise. There, I would see where I was and remember to keep time with Him a priority. Thank You, God!

Later in the day, as I thought about the experience, I realized I never acknowledged any of the cares that previously overloaded me. Yet somehow, they were gone. In those few minutes of worshipping God, putting my focus on His greatness, a transfer took place. All my concerns disappeared and were forgotten, not by God, but by me. The weight of them lifted off me, while the weight of His glory, His presence, came upon me.

My experience reminded me of Jesus' words recorded in Matthew 11:28-30 regarding the ease of His yoke and lightness of His burden. A "yoke" is equipment to do hard work. We need the yoke of Jesus that comes upon us in the Presence of God. Apart from Him, we can't do anything (John 15:5). There is only one way to live this life, with and in Him!

His presence is our Source!

CHAPTER EIGHT

The Communion of the Holy Spirit

But the Helper, the Holy Spirit, whom the Father will send in My name, He will teach you all things, and bring to your remembrance all things that I said to you. (John 14:26 & 27)

In this chapter, I want to share with you about the Holy Spirit's participation in our relationship with God. I desire that you will gain an understanding of the Person and purpose of the Holy Spirit. And be inspired to draw near to God as a result.

Many people ask, "If God is in heaven, then how does He communicate with us, and how is He here with us on earth"? In answer to that, I will start with this; there is a communion with God that He invites us to participate in with Him. This communion is the Source of God's involvement in our life. And, communion is something we can have or do with God.

It's interesting to me that communion comes from the word "commune," which means to spend time with a person or people. It is also closely related to the word "communicate." God communicates with us as we commune with Him. And, He communicates with us through the Holy Spirit.

Now let's look further into how the Holy Spirit participates in our relationship with God. In 2 Corinthians 13:14 the Apostle Paul closed his letter to the church at Corinth with this statement;

"The grace of the Lord Jesus Christ and the Love of God and the communion of the Holy Spirit be with you all. Amen."

Learning about this communion of the Holy Spirit mentioned here is a key to living in the secret place. Communion is like fellowship, and we fellowship with God through the communion or involvement of the Holy Spirit in our life. John 15:26 tells us that the Holy Spirit proceeds from the Father. He is God's Spirit, and He has been sent to dwell in us. You can study this out more in the Gospel of John Chapters 14 through 16. Jesus explains it perfectly. Afterward, He fulfilled His purpose to die on the Cross for us, was resurrected, then ascended to the right hand of the Father in heaven. He told His disciples He'd send a Helper, the Holy Spirit, Who would live in and empower us while we're on earth. The Holy Spirit was sent to us as a Helper. He helps us in our relationship with God.

It was God Who inspired Paul to write those words to the church, and it still applies to us today. God wants us to know that He desires that we all live in constant communion with Him. He never intended for us to live a life separate from His all-encompassing love and care.

I love this Scripture, and I speak it to people often. I do this because God's Word is powerful, and when we understand His Word and speak it out loud to ourselves or others, we are releasing the action of it into our lives. We want the action of the Holy Spirit in our life. His presence with us is how the activity of God works in our life.

The word "communion" used here in 2 Corinthians 13:14 comes from the Greek root word *"Koinonia,"* pronounced; *"koynohneeah,"* which has to do with partnership, participation, communication, distribution, and fellowship. These words help us understand the activity of the Holy Spirit. Now, think about the meaning of each of these words. Consider the action of the Holy Spirit in our lives in these ways as I replace the word "communion" with its descriptive. Through them, God is saying to us;

The partnership of the Holy Spirit be with you.

The participation of the Holy Spirit be with you.

The communication of the Holy Spirit be with you.

The distribution of the Holy Spirit be with you.

The fellowship of the Holy Spirit be with you.

Through these types of communion with the Holy Spirit, we can actively participate in what He is capable of doing in our life. As we cooperate with Him, we get to know God, our Father, and our relationship with Him deepens. We learn to yield to Him in exchange for His work of peace and strength in our lives.

The Holy Spirit is continually with us, and He is the communicator between God and us. We cannot know the things of God on our own. They are revealed to us as God works in our lives through the communion of the Holy Spirit. As Paul wrote to the Corinthians;

But as it is written: Eye has not seen, nor ear heard, nor have entered into the heart of man the things which God has prepared for those who love Him. But God has revealed them to us through His Spirit. For the Spirit searches all things, yes, the deep things of God. For what man knows the things of a man except the spirit of the man which is in him? Even so, no one knows the things of God except the Spirit of God. Now we have received not the spirit of the world, but the Spirit who is from God, that we might know the things that have been freely given to us by God. 1 Corinthians 2:9-12

We see another example in Matthew 16:15—17 when Jesus asked His disciples, "Who do you say that I am"? Peter answered, "You are the Christ, the Son of the living God." Jesus answered, saying, "Blessed are you Simon Bar-Jonah, for flesh and blood has not revealed this to you, but My Father who is in heaven." You see, only God could reveal to Peter, also known as Simon Bar-Jonah, that Jesus was the Christ, the Son of God, it was not something Peter figured out on his own. Knowing the truth about God only comes through the communion of the Holy Spirit, Who proceeds from the Father. He reveals the truth and causes us to comprehend the things of God.

Often people do not give God a chance to work in their life because they don't know Him or His desire to do good things on their behalf. Many people think things about God that are not true. Without ever having an encounter with God through the communion of the Holy Spirit, they have decided that what they think about God is a fact, and they live their lives devoid of a real relationship with Him.

So how do we cooperate with the Holy Spirit in this communion?

As you think of this Scripture in 2 Corinthians, turn your attention to God and acknowledge the presence of the Holy Spirit with you and thank God for His communion. As you do this, you are positioning yourself to interact with your heavenly Father. You are saying, "I see this in Your Word God, that you have sent the Holy Spirit to help me know You and I want to cooperate with You and get to know You in a very real way." Remember, God said if we seek Him, we will find Him (Jeremiah 29:13). So be willing to let God show you who He is. The more we are open to learning about God, the more He can reveal Himself to us and give us understanding in His ways. If you sincerely want to know Him and are willing to let Him show you Who He is, then you can receive from the communion of the Holy Spirit that is with you. He will make Himself known to you. And, as you study God's Word and make a continual effort to know Him, the Holy Spirit will be with you giving you understanding and guiding you on your journey of living in the secret place of God's presence.

Remember the words that describe communion and let the Holy Spirit operate in you. Partner and participate with Him. Allow Him to communicate the revelation knowledge of God to your spirit and distribute His character in and through you to others. Enjoy His fellowship!

He is the best friend you will ever have in this life.

CHAPTER NINE

From a Prayer Life to a Life of Prayer

Be anxious for nothing, but in everything by prayer and supplication, with thanksgiving, let your requests be made known to God. (Phil. 4:6 & 7)

Have you ever heard people talk about their prayer life as if it is a separate part of their life? Well, early on in our walk with God, our prayer life starts that way. We spend time in prayer, and then we run off with our day, never applying what we learned or thinking about God again until the next prayer time. But God desires to walk with us throughout our day, every day. That way, who we are with God privately is also who we are in public. I like to say we go from having a prayer life, to having a life of prayer. Yes, this is possible, and God is ready to show us how and give us the desire and ability to do it.

I realized one day that what goes on in my private prayer time was meant to overflow in every area of my life. And, I wanted that to be a reality. So, I turned to God with my desire and purposed in my heart to learn how. My determination took me on a journey of transforming my prayer life into a life of prayer.

A life of prayer doesn't mean we stay in our prayer closet all day. But that through what happens there, we become more mindful of our relationship with God, and we don't separate ourselves from Him when we leave our meeting place. We learn to develop continual communication between His heart and ours. Then, no matter where we are, there's an awareness of Him with us at all times.

During our private prayer, God makes things known to us, sometimes without us even realizing the depth of it. Then as we go about our day, the word He impressed upon our heart in private is confirmed by an experience He orchestrates for us, which is one of the ways He reveals that He is with us, guiding us through life. It is the outflow of living from the secret place.

When we begin, most likely, we will experience wonderful times alone with God, then go out into the activities of our day and mess up a whole bunch. Sometimes we find it challenging to return to our prayer closet and face God. We've all been there, so please make a quality decision now, never to allow the difficulty to stop you from returning to Him in your prayer closet. It's not like God won't know if you don't tell Him. He knows everything, all of our mistakes and shortcomings, yet He loves us anyway. He wants us to come running to Him, so He can cleanse us from any guilt or condemnation and get us recharged in His presence. Then we are ready to go out and try again. Our transformation is a process. Ask God to help you notice times when you run off and do things leaving your awareness of Him in your closet. Be mindful of taking Him with you everywhere.

As we learn to live in the secret place, the attention of our heart stays toward God. He is our Source for everything! In every situation, we should quickly run to or turn our attention to Him for help, comfort, cleansing, forgiveness, ability, wisdom, insight, strength, rest, everything! No matter what, we look to God.

As we keep this pattern of living, we will become less self-focused or self-dependent and more dependent on God, which is a good thing. Really, it is extremely freeing not to be focused on ourselves. The more opportunity we give God to work in us, the more we will live in the secret place, the place of His presence where His help is active in our lives. As we develop a habit of always looking to Him, the self-centered part of us bows to the majesty of God, and our lives will go so much better.

As you know, life can be boisterous and busy at times. Since we are developing a life of prayer, we may, at times, have to physically separate ourselves from a current situation to find a quiet place to be with God so that we can hear Him and get the help we need. Remember Moses had to pitch his tent outside the camp away from the people to hear from God (Exodus 33:1—11).

Picture this. God and you are going into a massive storm. A fierce wind is blowing, and it's pouring down rain. The noise is so loud you can't hear anything but the rain. You're carrying an umbrella, but you're fighting with it through the storm. Because of the conditions, you can't hear the Lord's instructions as you are trying to follow Him. He's telling you to hold your umbrella a certain way so it will protect you. Instead, you are thinking, throw your umbrella away, it can't protect you. He reveals a covered area to you where you can get out of the rain and wind. It's quiet, and you can now hear what He is saying. He fixes your umbrella, you catch your breath, refocus, and then He instructs you to go out again. This time you are better acquainted with His ways, and you make it through the rest of the storm much easier.

It is a matter of the attention of our hearts toward God. If this is what we sincerely desire, then we can ask God to help us turn our prayer life into a life of prayer, and He will. Soon, no matter what is going on around us, our hearts will be steadfast, trusting in the Lord. We will be able to quietly enter that secret place of communion with the Father wherever we are, and He will lead us through everything we encounter.

I see this as "dwelling in the secret place of the Most High," and there we abide under His all-encompassing love and care.

CHAPTER TEN

His Word, Our Guide

*Your word is a lamp to my feet and
a light to my path.* (Ps. 119:105)

The Bible is God's Word to us. It's the history of what He has done and the promise of what He will do. It's the words of His heart that He wants us to know so that we will have the guidance needed in life.

If we make studying the Bible a part of our private prayer time with God, we can learn His way of doing things. Then if we apply what we learn, it will help us in every area of our life. It will help us stay aware of Him, and it will guide us in every situation. Think about this; the word "guide" has to do with showing someone the way or having an influence on someone's or something's course of action. As we go about our day, God's Word and His Spirit are with us, ready to guide us. If we choose to follow God and act upon His guidance, we can experience great peace and strength and enjoy the good God has planned for us.

Psalm 119:105 tells us that God's Word is a "lamp unto our feet and light unto our path."

You see, God doesn't want us to live without His help. He gave us the instruction of His Word so we can know what to do and what not to do. Let me share some examples with you. Here's a favorite Scripture of mine from Philippians 4:6 and 7 that helps me navigate life;

"Be anxious for nothing, but in everything by prayer and supplication, with thanksgiving, let your request be made known to God; And the peace of God, which surpasses all understanding, will guard your hearts and minds through Christ Jesus."

This Scripture shows us how to exchange anxiety for peace.

I use to focus on the part that reads, "Be anxious for nothing," in other translations, it reads, "don't worry about anything." I tried so hard not to worry about things, but as hard as I tried, I wasn't making much progress in this area. Then in my desperation of wanting to obey God by not worrying, I asked Him for His help, and He showed me what I was missing.

You see, we can't just make ourselves not worry or be anxious. We shouldn't be ashamed of any anxiety or worry, either. It is a natural reaction to things we deal with in life, and God knows that. He is telling us in this Scripture that when we are anxious, we don't have to stay worried. We can do something about it. We can take our worries to Him in exchange for His peace and be relieved of the anxiety.

I was so focused on what not to do, "Be anxious for nothing," that I hadn't noticed the next bit of instruction that revealed what I was to do. It was found in the next part of the verse, "in everything by prayer and supplication, with thanksgiving, let your request be known to God."

"Let our request be known to God" means to talk with God in prayer, request, or ask for His help in your areas of concern. He wants to help with everything. Our asking is like an invitation to Him, an invitation He will gladly accept. He knows what is needed in every situation and has the best plan to take care of it. Most times, He takes a different route in resolving the issues in our life than what we would think to do, but as we continue to thank Him for taking care of things, His way, we will see the best results.

Here's how Psalm 119:105 becomes a reality in our life. "God's Word is the lamp unto our feet and the light unto our path."

When we are dealing with things that cause anxiousness or worry, Philippians 4:6 and 7 becomes the lamp and light to guide us. It instructs us to turn to God. And, with a thankful attitude, pray to Him about the things that are concerning us. As we turn our attention to God and begin to pray, we are reminded He is for us. We thank Him for His faithfulness and lift our concerns to Him, asking for His help. We may even think about how He worked things out in previous situations and thank Him for that. These are our testimonies, and they encourage us to lean on Him even more in the current situation. As we do this, an exchange takes place. And, our concerns are released into His care, knowing He has heard our prayer. He then concerns Himself with the things we talk with Him about, as the rest of the verse becomes a reality. "The peace of God" comes to our aid. His peace flows from the relationship we have with Him, and it fills our hearts and minds, which is one of the benefits of living in the secret place. So beautiful are the ways of God!

The Books of Psalm and Proverbs are great parts of the Bible to learn basic principles for everyday life. Making this part of your daily study will help you grow in marvelous ways. Here is an example from Proverbs 3 that I find very useful. As you look at this Scripture, notice the instructions the Word gives us, and then the awesome results of applying them. See how our God cares for us!

"Trust in the Lord with all your heart, and lean not on your own understanding; In all your ways acknowledge Him, and He will direct your paths." Proverbs 3:5 and 6

His instruction here is helpful when situations arise where we lack understanding and don't know what to do. Notice in this verse, there are two key things we are "to do," one "not to do," then the result we get as we follow His instructions.

Do: Trust in the Lord and acknowledge Him in all your ways.
Don't: Lean not on your own understanding.
Result: God will direct your steps.

God wants to guide us through life, and He will give us direction for every step if we look to Him for help.

You may find that you struggle to trust God. Your ability to trust God can be cultivated as you study the Bible. As we study God's Word, we can see God's faithfulness recorded throughout the Scriptures, and we come to realize He is trustworthy.

As we apply this Scripture in Proverbs, our degree of trusting God will increase as we begin to acknowledge Him and see how He moves on our behalf.

You see, when we acknowledge that God is our God, knowing that He is far superior than we are and knows far more than we do, we remember He is trustworthy. He is just in all His ways, He is for us, and we can trust Him. He cares about our well-being and knows how to get us moving in the right direction. When we are struggling and confused about why things are happening the way they are, we can turn our focus to God, remember how good He is and acknowledge Him as the One who watches over us. He can guide us through anything. As we recognize God this way, the soulish part of us settles down in a trusted state of mind so that we can begin looking expectantly for God to direct us. And He will!

His direction can come in different ways, but we can tell when the direction we are sensing is from God because it will line up with the principals of His Word.

Remember, His Word is our Guide. When we are dealing with the activities of our day, the Holy Spirit will bring to our remembrance the things we've been learning. He will make suggestions on how we can apply the principles of God's Word to what we are doing. As we use them, we will have the results God intends for us.

Knowing the Word of God and applying it as our guide is a secret to living in the secret place.

CHAPTER ELEVEN

Responding to God

When You said, "Seek My face," My heart said to You, "Your face, Lord, I will seek." (Ps 27:8)

Another secret to living in the secret place is learning to respond to God.

Understanding how to respond to God starts by listening and answering God in private prayer. As we begin to answer Him in prayer, we learn to follow Him in our daily activities. Prayer is an invitation to God to get involved in our life. However, He will only be involved to the degree we allow Him by our response. It's a reciprocal relationship. We call, He answers. He calls, we answer. Our response will always move God's heart. If we stop responding to Him, the ball is in our court, so to say. He patiently waits for us to return to Him regarding His last action.

You may look at some people and say, "Wow, God is really with them." It may seem God loves or favors some more than others, but what you may be witnessing is His response to those who respond to Him. He never forces Himself on us. He allows us to decide how much we want to be with Him. If it has been a long time since you responded to God, He is eagerly waiting for you to reach out to Him. A sincere turn of your heart toward Him will get the ball rolling again. The relationship between you and God can be renewed anytime. And, when you do, His peace will flood your heart and mind again.

Stop now and turn back to Him if you have been away. Ask God to forgive you and pray this prayer from Psalm 51:10-12. He will renew you!

"Create in me a clean heart Oh God, and renew a steadfast spirit within me. Do not cast me away from Your Presence and do not take Your Holy Spirit from me. Restore to me the joy of Your salvation and uphold me with Your generous Spirit."

RESPONDING TO THE PROMPTINGS OF GOD

Part of living in the secret place is keeping our attention on God so we can pick up on His guidance in our life. Remember from the previous chapter, His guidance will always line up with the principles of His Word. He guides us with certain feelings or thought-provoking impressions we may have from time to time. I like to call these His promptings.

It can be challenging at times to keep our attention on God when we are outside of our prayer closet. Many things distract us, but as we learn how He prompts us, we can respond in a way that keeps our communion with Him close no matter where we are.

WHAT ARE THE PROMPTINGS OF GOD?

Part of the Holy Spirit's communion is to move on us in such a way that we recognize it to be God drawing our attention toward someone or something. Remember, the Holy Spirit is God in us, and He is an ever-present help to us.

Promptings are the Holy Spirit suggesting that our spirit gives attention to God. He knows where our heart is focused and what is ahead in our lives. He wants to guide us through everything, but we have to stay in communion with Him to recognize His promptings. He will help us with this. He goes before us, and He will tell us of things to come (John 16:13). If we are listening to Him, we will be ready to respond to His guidance. He will navigate us through challenging circumstances and lead us into places of rest and replenishment. Along the way, we can experience joyful fellowship with Him.

He knows all things. He knows the end from the beginning and has already been where He is taking us. He has overcome all things, and if we walk with Him, we too will overcome all things. It is in Him that we live and move and have our being (Acts 17:28).

Let me share a couple of examples from my experience with the promptings of God.

THE PROMPTING TO DRAW NEAR TO GOD

The prompting of God sometimes comes as a desire toward Him or a longing to give Him our full attention. It might be that you want to spend some quiet time with Him, reading the Word or slipping into your prayer closet to make yourself available to Him to pray for someone or something. It may be that you are not to say or do anything but bow down before Him in reverence of His presence with you. When you notice a longing within you like this, don't ignore it. Respond to God.

For instance, the desire to bow down before God is an act of worship that shouldn't be limited to our scheduled prayer times or when we are gathered as a congregation. It may be your habit to bow beside your bed upon waking or before lying down to sleep. These are appropriate times, and God is honored when we bow before Him. However, sometimes the presence of God will suddenly be strong upon you, and you have to stop whatever it is you are doing, and at that very moment, acknowledge Him by bowing down in response to Him. He is Worthy!

These desires toward God arise in us because of the relationship we have with Him. If we respond, it enhances our communion with Him and establishes a deeper union with Him. It is God prompting us to allow His Presence to flow and accomplish His will.

We are living in days when the world needs to experience the presence and power of God that comes through the lives of those who know Him. We must learn to walk in the place where God's presence is manifested to the degree that it impacts every atmosphere we encounter and ignites every heart around us to know Him. I believe the day is coming when unbelievers will fall on their knees in front of us and cry out to know our God.

Moments like these are what happens as we live our lives from the secret place with God.

THE PROMPTING TO PRAY

Another way God prompts us is through a prompting to pray. Sometimes I will say, "So and so is on my heart," meaning they are on my mind, and I cannot stop thinking of them. I have learned that this is a prompting by the Holy Spirit to pray. You get a sense the person on your mind needs help. You may not know what it is, but you sense there is a need that requires prayer. The Spirit of God is getting our attention because He knows what is going on. He is looking for someone to pray and ask for His help to be released into their lives. Oh, how God loves us!

If we want to be available to the Lord our God for prayer, we will get these promptings. We respond by turning our attention to Him and allowing the Holy Spirit to reveal to us what to pray. Then let Him continue to lead you through a prayer of intercession or supplication until you feel a release in your heart. Intercession means you are intervening on behalf of another person. Supplication happens when you earnestly ask God to supply whatever the person needs. I love how God does this.

Sometimes there is no specific person or thing on our mind, but there is a sense of a need to pray. In this case, turn your attention to God and begin to make yourself available to Him by exalting Him with words of praise and declaration of His worthiness and almightiness. As you narrow your focus on

Him, you become ready to hear Him and follow Him in prayer. Then He, by His Spirit, will reveal to you the things that need to be prayed so you can respond by speaking these things out to Him in prayer and requesting His help. He hears our prayer and responds. These prayers are directed from the heart of God. As a result, He releases His power into the situations He has prompted us to lift up in our prayers. Amazing!!

As we learn to become more aware of God working in this way, we will become more alert and ready to hear and respond to His promptings to pray. This awareness of Him and responding to Him is one of the ways we live in the secret place.

I remember a time when the Lord was teaching me about His promptings to pray. I was on my way to work one day. I had a forty-five-minute commute, which was often a time of prayer for me. My attention was on the Lord, and somewhere along the way of prayer, I began praying for the people at work. To my surprise, I found myself praying for a lady at work and requesting healing for her. She wasn't someone I saw every day and had very little interaction with, but there she was in my prayers. I remember wondering why I had prayed for her because I was not aware of anything about her. I continued with my prayer time and didn't give it any more thought.

Later that day, I walked into the break room, and there she was getting something to drink. Another person was in the room, and as I walked in, I heard the other person ask the lady how she was feeling. She replied that she was much better but still not quite one hundred percent. I didn't say a word, but I realized, at that moment, it was the Lord that prompted me to pray for her, and because of His prayer, she would fully recover. Praise God!

I believe God had me hear that conversation in the break room, not so I could tell her I prayed for her (which I did not do), but so I would know He prompted my prayer, and He was working in me and teaching me His ways.

There are times the Lord will prompt us to let someone know God had us pray for them. If the Lord inspires me to tell someone, I was praying for them; it is not so they will thank me and think I'm something great. It is so they will know God loves them so much and was aware of their need and moved on their behalf to find someone He could empower with a prayer for them. He is Amazing!

If we are not living in the secret place, we can miss these promptings. I wonder how many prayers have not been prayed because someone wasn't listening.

When we pray, God gets involved. As we live in the secret place of communion with Him, we will learn to respond to the things we encounter with a listening ear to God, hearing His promptings to pray. Then He can release His Kingdom power into the lives of those in need.

The prompting to draw near to God and the prompting to pray are just a couple of ways God will move in our life as we endeavor to live in the secret place of communion with Him. Take notice when you are thinking of God and remember that it is Him prompting you. Then respond to Him in a way that draws your attention towards Him allowing Him to lead you in an incredible and eternally valuable activity.

CHAPTER TWELVE

The Joyful Process

*And now my head shall be lifted up above
my enemies all around me; Therefore, I will offer
sacrifices of joy in His tabernacle; I will sing, yes,
I will sing praises to the Lord.* (Ps. 27:6)

I remember when I was first discovering the joy of spending time alone with God and how it began to change the way I felt about everything. My relationship with Him started when someone shared with me about how Jesus died for me so that I could live forever with God in Heaven. As a young child, I heard that God existed and that when our life was finished here on earth, we would spend eternity, either with God in Heaven or without Him in hell. But I didn't know what determined where we would go. I was so grateful to learn that if I asked Jesus to come into my life and be my Lord, He would, and as a result, I would spend eternity in Heaven with Him.

Later I was given a Bible and taken to a church that taught the importance of studying God's Word. I grew to love the Scriptures. The Bible became my go-to manual for everything.

One day I discovered the Scriptures that revealed how to find God by seeking Him (Deuteronomy 4:29 & Jeremiah

29:13). There was something big in me to know God. Not just know about Him but to know Him as a personal friend. I was around people who seemed to know Him that way, and I wondered if it was possible for me.

When I found those verses, I took the desire in my heart and pursued a close relationship with God. I believed it was possible and set the attention of my thoughts toward discovering God's way of thinking. I wanted to know Who He was to me and who I was to Him. So hungry to know Him, I read my Bible as much as I could. I participated in small group Bible studies, church services, and fellowships watching to see how people lived who seemed to know Him. When I got an understanding of the Scriptures and learned that God wanted something a certain way, then that was the way I wanted it too. It was a process, but the more I spent time with God, the more I wanted to spend time with Him, and the more I got to know Him.

Incredible things take place during our time alone with God. He helps us deal with past pains and hurts to heal our wounds and make us free to enjoy the life He has in store for us. In those precious times alone with Him, I learned I could trust Him, and with His help, I found out who I thought I was and who God said I was. Noticing the discrepancies, I made choices to change the way I thought about myself so that my thinking would agree with the way God thought about me. Wow, what a journey of discovery, healing, forgiveness, and transformation.

It was through those times alone with God that I found He not only wants us to know Him, but He wants us to live in this secret place of His presence continually. If we respond to the opportunities He puts before us, we can learn to live there.

God created us with a desire for us to have a close relationship. As we find that connection with Him, we become more and more like clay in His hands, trusting Him to work things out in ways, we could never do on our own. Life's journey with Him beautifully unfolds as joy and strength fill our life. It compels us to keep looking to Him concerning everything, yes, everything. In the process, we become free of worry, fear, and frustration and full of peace and stability. The more we discover, the more we want to know Him. Oh, what a joy to know our God!

If you have discovered that secret place with God, you know what I am talking about and I want to encourage you to pursue Him all the more for an even deeper walk with Him. If you have not yet discovered that secret place with God, then know that He wants that with you also. Pursue Him, and you will be amazed at the secrets awaiting your discovery.

Oh, how beautiful your life will be.

CHAPTER THIRTEEN

Closing

There is so much more in a relationship with God than I could ever explain, but as I wrote earlier, I hope that what I have shared will inspire you to find your place with God, court His presence and enjoy the life He has for you.

I wonder if you noticed while reading this book that the focus began about our individual relationship with God then transitioned to include an outward concern for others. You see, as we continue to practice these principles, keeping close to God through our one on One communion with Him, we experience His incredible love, and something happens in the depth of our being. We can't help but want others to know Him too. As God reveals Himself and we unveil ourselves, the communion of His heart and ours invades every part of us and transforms our inward focus. The transformation of our inward focus brings about a deep compassion for others. The wellspring of God within us releases the fire of His Spirit in a flame of desire for others to know Him. As we continue in Him, He moves in our interactions with others, allowing an opportunity for them to discover the love we have found. It is only in our God that true freedom can be experienced. His presence brings to our very being the peace and strength our heart desires. I hope that as you endeavor to live in this secret place, discovering the heart of God, you too will want to be sure everyone around you knows Him, and these truths will be passed on from generation to generation.

Now, may I, as an ambassador for Christ, as though God were pleading through me, implore you on Christ's behalf, to live from the secret place of God's presence. Carry with you the peace and strength He gives you. Be ready to hear and follow His promptings along the way, and be a part of bringing the kingdom of heaven to earth so that others can know Him too. Experiencing that joy is a secret unlocked.

Let me end by praying this prayer over you:

Dear Father, You see the heart of the one who is reading these words, I ask in the name of Jesus that You would grant to them the ability to learn of You. Please release the communion of Your Holy Spirit into their life that they may experience how much You love them and how they can enjoy every good and perfect gift You have prepared for them. Teach them Your ways, oh God, and help them to walk with You to the fullness that You intend for them. Free them from every restraint that has kept them from knowing You and fill them with Your peace. Let them experience times in Your manifest presence that sets their heart aflame for You. And from this day forward, may they live a life of ever-increasing joy and strength. And may they know for sure that when they reach the end of their days on earth, they will experience the joy of Your eternal Glory. Thank You, Father, for hearing my prayer. Amen.

Now my friend, go and live in the "Secret Place of God's Presence!"

About the Author

Serving in ministry for over 30 years in different capacities, Barbara A. Michael has always found herself drawn to people of prayer. With a passion to see others grow in the knowledge of God and walk in close communion with Him, she makes the most of every opportunity to help others experience His love and presence. Through teaching in a precept and example format, she aspires to help people find their way to close communion with God as they experience prayer to the Father to be as easy as breathing.

Barbara has served as a ministry leader, elder, and associate pastor over the years and now serves as Minister and Founder of Living by Prayer, a ministry launched in 2016 with the purpose of releasing the kingdom of God on the earth through prayer. The ministry includes teaching and leading a variety of prayer assemblies, including city-wide meetings that cross denominational lines to help bring unity in the Body of Christ in order to reach communities with the gospel.

With a fervent desire to see God's people living as true ambassadors for Jesus Christ, demonstrating the kingdom of heaven on earth and carrying out the command of Jesus to make disciples of all nations, Barbara sets her affections on

Christ and endeavors to humbly serve Him every day, knowing that apart from Him she can do nothing.

Barbara and her husband Raymond, who introduced her to Jesus many years ago, reside in Florida, close to their family.

To reach Barbara and find out more about the Living by Prayer ministry visit: barbaramichael.org